ARCHITECTURAL ORNAMENTATION IN CHICAGO

ARCHITECTURAL ORNAMENTATION IN CHICAGO

WILLIAM A. ROONEY

CHICAGO REVIEW PRESS, CHICAGO

Every element of architectural
ornament originates with an artist's
sketch or model. Artisans then take
over, translating these ideas into stone,
cast concrete, terra cotta, metal or
other material. It is the skilled work of
these nameless artisans that we pass by
each day, admiring it or ignoring it. To
these unknown artisans let this book be
dedicated.

Library of Congress Cataloging in Publication Data

Rooney, William A.
Architectural ornamentation in Chicago.

1. Decoration and ornament, Architectural — Illinois —
Chicago.   2. Chicago (Ill.) — Description.   I. Title.
NA3511.C4R66   1984   729'.09773'11   84-15546
ISBN 0-914091-38-7
ISBN 0-914091-39-5   (pbk.)

Published by Chicago Review Press, Chicago

CONTENTS

INTRODUCTION

This is a book of pictures which record exterior architectural ornament in the greater Chicago area.

Nothing is more absurd than to use one medium of communication — words — to describe another medium — architectural ornament. Accordingly, aside from this introduction and some paragraphs of explanation to open each chapter, pictures are used to tell the story of the richness of the architectural ornament to be found in Chicago. Churches and theaters, with a few exceptions, are excluded from this study. Church architectural ornament is a study of its own. Theater decoration and ornament, as characterized by the motion picture palaces of Chicago, likewise is so special as to warrant separate coverage. To cover these forms in this book would mean that almost all other architectural ornament would be overshadowed.

Chicago is one of the richest lodes of architectural ornament in America. Every ornamental form has been expressed. Every medium has been used — stone, cast concrete, terra cotta, metal, brick. The labors of every kind of artist and artisan have been combined to create and execute the ornament. It is somewhat tragic that so much effort has gone into this ornament only to have it be so casually accepted by those who pass by. Indeed, an enormous quantity of splendid ornament is so placed as to be invisible to man, whose life it was intended to enrich. No end of ornament can be seen only from the street with binoculars or from windows of upper floors of buildings across the way.

What prompts such a book as this? Moving about the city in the course of a day's routine, slowly but surely the ornament to be seen begins to impress itself on the mind of the viewer. Unaware that he is doing so, that viewer begins to recognize and classify what he is seeing: there is another coach light, this time in brass, not in wrought iron. As visual images build and group themselves in the mind, the moment at last arrives when a conscious urge is felt somehow to record, assemble and store them. The result: out comes the camera and the search begins in earnest.

Let no reader expect this to be a learned book on architectural ornament. It is not. And let no reader expect this book to be offered as an historical document which sets out to preserve in pictures a record of the ornament which will be — or has been — the victim of the wrecker's ball. That ball so indiscriminately destroys architectural efforts — good or bad — that there is no keeping up with it, nor does there seem to be any force that can stay its work. Further, let no one regard this volume as a comprehensive record of ornament in Chicago. Any such concept is impossible despite the author's original intention to "get all of this down." When the actual photo shooting is launched, the impossibility of a comprehensive effort is revealed.

To begin, what is ornament? The best definition in the context of architecture seems to be this one by Christopher Dresser, written in 1862:

Ornament is that which superadded to utility, renders the object more acceptable through bestowing upon it an amount of beauty which it would not otherwise possess.
(From "The Art of Design," p. 1, to be found in *Ornament*, from VIA III, published by the Graduate School of Fine Arts, University of Pennsylvania, 1977.)

Another question surfaces: Why architectural ornament? There appear to be three answers to this question: (1) to break up the lines of the building, (2) to allow the architect to affix his imprint on the building, and (3) to identify and give honor to the owner of the building. There is, perhaps, no end of other reasons. Accordingly, another reason might be tradition. The Chinese temple entrance was originally guarded by live dogs. Later, the temple dog became a statue. The ancient Celt was known to affix the head of his victim on a pike and post it outside the door of his dwelling. Every culture has marked its dwellings with some form of ornament either for utilitarian or for decorative purpose. The modern architect has borrowed from all cultures to bring ornament to his finished work. Chapter 6 of this book shows how even the architect who designs in steel, glass and concrete along such austere lines as would do credit to Piet Mondrian, now defies the austerity of his own design in order to bring some form of artistic expression — by way of ornament — to his work.

Curiously, industries have been established to mass produce architectural ornament. Forms of flora and geometric designs could be ordered by the foot out of a catalog in America as early as the 1860's. Companies in this business flourished up to the 1930's. Most, if not all, of them have vanished. With all this mass production of ornament, it is puzzling that stock ornament does not repeat itself more often on buildings in greater Chicago. It is a fact, however, that over a period of 10 years of continuous observation and photographing of architectural ornament, only a handful of duplicated ornaments have been found.

Ornament is not duplicated in Chicago, but its *forms* are repeated. That is what much of this book is about. It is interesting and at the same time amusing that ornamental forms are so often repeated that they can be categorized, as has been done in this book. At the same time, the architect, artist and artisan must be credited for finding such infinite variety with which to express these forms. Ornament on a single building can fall into a number of categories (the human figure, animals, coach lights, etc.). In such cases, the building is represented in this book as often as this is appropriate. No building is so humble that the architect, the owner or the builder did not find a way to ornament it if he were so inclined. Any number of the most modest buildings in Chicago are interestingly ornamented, and that ornament is included in this volume.

As noted earlier, this collection of photographs was not made for some erudite purpose. It was done for the fun of it. There is a special, secret inner pleasure in collecting these examples of ornamentation and sharing them with others who appreciate our architectural heritage. Simply seeing them and storing them away in the mind as a personal treasure isn't enough. They need to be photographed, gathered into a single place and shared. If such collecting contributes something worthwhile, that is welcome.

The author is indebted to Robert
Buchbinder and R. Timothy Rooney for
providing photos used in this book.
They were kind enough to furnish the
following pictures: Robert Buchbinder:
Chapter 1, opening picture and no. 23;
Chapter 4, no. 11; Chapter 6, no.
1; Chapter 8, nos. 19, 20, 21, 22; Chapter
9, nos. 17, 18, 19, 20; Chapter 15, no.
22; Chapter 16, no. 39. R. Timothy
Rooney: Chapter 1, nos. 12, 22, 37;
Chapter 2, nos. 1, 3, 7, 8, 9, 11, 12, 13,
15, 16, 18, 23, 24, 26, 28, 31, 32, 33, 35,
36,37,38; Chapter 5, no.6; Chapter
10, opening picture; Chapter 14, no. 17.

Big Game Hunting

In architecture, the lion is far from an endangered species. Rather, it is ubiquitous; it may be found at any elevation. It may be in plain view or stealthily hiding. It may be found front and center as a corporate symbol (Harris Trust) or as a simple decorative element lost in other designs. The lion is intended to represent all that is strong and courageous. As with the temple dog in the Chinese culture, live lions guarded the temple entrance in other societies. The lion perhaps found its way into architectural ornament from that beginning. Outside Beirut, ancient Roman ruins at Ballbek display the lion head — one example of the extent to which this form of ornament traces back into history.

Felis Leo appears in almost every construction or ornamental medium, from metal and stone to terra cotta. While it may be seen full form (Harris Trust, Art Institute), the lion's head has been most frequently used by the architect. Some architects have not been content with just one head design per building, repeating it around the facade. Occasionally the architect has used multiple lion head designs — as many as three, for example, on the 208 South LaSalle St. Building. Interestingly, two different lion head forms stare down at the pair of lions guarding the Art Institute, two of Chicago's more widely known landmarks. Those lions which enjoy the higher ground (without appropriate recognition) are on the People's Gas Light & Coke Building, 122 S. Michigan Ave.

Big game hunting discloses that the panther heads on the push plates of the revolving doors of the Marquette Building (#39) were designed by the sculptor of the Art Institute lions, Edward Kemeys.

Majestic Office Bldg.
22 W Monroe St.

1

5

1. 208 S. LaSalle St.
2. 1508 N. State St.
3. 1254 Lake Shore Dr.
4. 531 Grove St., Evanston
5. Crerar Library, 83 E. Randolph (demolished)
6. 63 E. Adams St.
7. McVickers Theater, 25 W. Madison St.

3

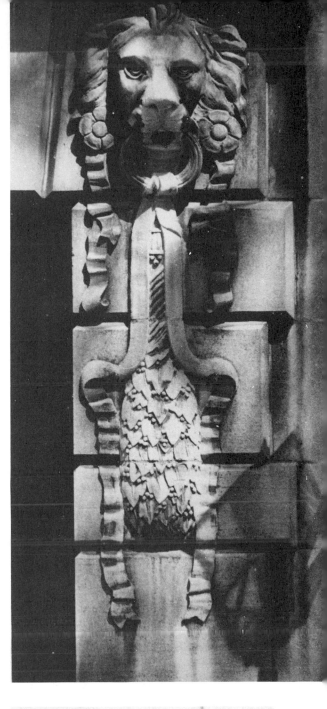

4

6

7

8

9

10

12

13

11

15

4

16

17. St. Clair Hotel, 162 E. Ohio
18. 1430 Chicago Ave., Evanston
19. Commonwealth Edison Bldg., Adams and Clark
20, 21. Peoples Gas Company Bldg., 122 S. Michigan
22. Sherman House, Randolph and Clark (demolished)
23. Handplate, revolving door, Marquette Bldg.,
    140 S. Dearborn St.

21

22

18

19

20

23

24

25

28

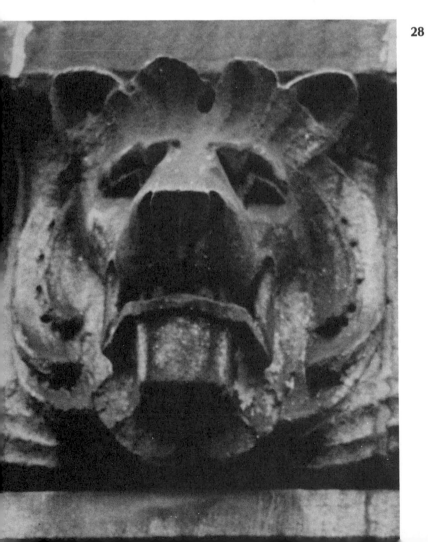

29

26

27

30

31

24. 1520 N. State St.
25. Abandoned bridge,
    Illinois Highway 59 at Golf Rd.
26. Chicago Cultural Center,
    Michigan Ave. and Randolph St.
27. Douglas Park Auditorium,
    3200 W. Ogden
28. 208 S.LaSalle St.
29. 728 N. Michigan Ave.
30. 203 N. Wabash Ave.
31. Dewes House,
    503 W. Wrightwood Ave.

32. Peoples Gas Company Bldg.,
    122 S. Michigan Ave. (top of bldg.)
33. 627 Eleventh St., Wilmette
34. YMCA Bldg., 19 S. LaSalle St.
35. Hahn Bldg.,
    1609 Orrington, Evanston
36. 40 N. Wells St.
37. Art Institute,
    S. Michigan and E. Adams St.
38. 100 W. Chicago Ave.

33

34

36

37

38

The Coach Light

Distinctive elements of architectural ornament are the instruments of illumination found at building entrances. *Coach Light* is the term for this ornamental form, and usually they are found in pairs. The form and the word *coach* derive from Kocs, a city in Hungary where the "coach" vehicle first became popular. The coach was a closed, horse-drawn, wheeled vehicle accommodating at least four passengers inside, with doors in the middle of the sides. It dates from the middle 16th century.

Building entrance coach lights probably originated with this vehicle. Lanterns that the coach carried to light the road were demountable so they could be used upon night arrival to light stable or courtyard while horses were posted for the night.

Other forms of building entrance illumination had their origins elsewhere. Contemporary lanterns hanging from chains may have had their beginnings as lanterns thrown over the castle wall to show who was seeking entrance to the fortress in the night. Further, the imagination can picture the concierge at an inn or hostel lighting a faggot and hanging it in an iron bracket outside the entrance to burn through the night to light the way for the weary night traveler. In its original form, the coach light was a sign of hospitality. Carried over to the present, this is evidenced by the frequency of coach lights being seen today at entrances of hotels, restaurants and hospitals.

The architect has employed the coach light for ornament rather than for illumination since few coach lights found today on buildings give off no more than the meanest glow.

As with other architectural ornament, no structure is too prestigious or too humble to be decorated with coach lights. Perhaps the most magnificent set of such lights to be found in Chicago is that which illuminates the entrance to the McCormick Building at 332 South Michigan Ave. The most humble building to bear a coach light is a tiny pie-shaped structure off an alley-like street in Wilmette. The building was once the village street lighting plant and is now the property of Commonwealth Edison.

llinois Bell Telephone Bldg.
12 W. Washington

1

2

3

4

6

7

8

1. Willoughby Tower,
   8 S. Michigan Ave.
2. Bankers Bldg.,
   105 W. Adams St.
3. Illinois Bell Telephone Bldg.,
   311 W. Washington St.
4. Moody Church,
   1630 N. Clark
5. Central National Bank Bldg.,
   171 W. Monroe St.
6. 1500 Lake Shore Dr.,
   (Burton Pl. entrance)
7. Commonwealth Edison Substation,
   S.W. corner Ontario St.
   and Dearborn Ave.
8. Materials Service Corporation Bldg.,
   300 W. Washington St.
9. 10 S. LaSalle St.
10. Hahn Bldg.,
    1609 Orrington Ave., Evanston

9

10

11

STATE OF ILLINOIS

12

15

16

17

13

14

20

19

21

22

23

26

27

21. 1200 N. Lake Shore Dr.
22. 1500 N. Lake Shore Dr.
    (Lake Shore Dr. entrance)
23. Crerar Library Bldg.,
    83 E. Randolph St. (demolished)
24. Commonwealth Edison Substation,
    Central St., Wilmette
25. Jackson—Franklin Bldg.,
    309 W. Jackson St.
26. Amphitheater,
    4200 S. Halsted (removed)
27. 1430 N. Lake Shore Dr.
28. Pittsfield Bldg.,
    55 E. Washington St.
29. Passavant Hospital Bldg.,
    Superior and Fairbanks Ct.
30. 1410 N. LaSalle St.

24

25

30

8

29

31

35 36

31. Conrad Hilton Hotel,
720 S. Michigan Ave.
32. 35 E. Wacker
33. Randolph and Canal St.
34. Monadnock Bldg.,
54 W. Van Buren St. entrance
35. McCormick Bldg.,
332 S. Michigan Ave.
36. Illinois Bell Telephone Bldg.,
641 N. Dearborn St.
37. LaSalle Hotel,
LaSalle and Madison St. (demolished)
38. State of Illinois Bldg.,
Randolph and LaSalle (Randolph entrance)

32

33

34

38

37

Armor and the Warrior

Imagery, thought to have been an invention of the advertising man, was in the architect's kit long before advertising types discovered the word. Architects and builders used imagery as symbols to give personality to the structures they built. One image they often sought to convey was that of strength, seriousness of purpose, permanence and/or sturdiness, and sometimes they achieved it by representing elements of armor or implements of war. Perhaps it was thought that armor provided a forbidding, even threatening image for the building it ornamented. Oddly, in some instances such imagery conveys the opposite of what should have been intended. For example, hospitality, warmth and welcome should be represented in the ornament of a hotel. Yet some of Chicago's most forbidding armor and implements of war decorate the Conrad Hilton (originally the Stevens Hotel). The same applies to an apartment building at 233 DeWitt. Few buildings seem more benign than the Insurance Center Building at 330 S. Wells, yet a medieval knight's armor and shield provide the building's key decorative element.

But the Greek and Roman spear, sheaf of arrows, body plate and shield are not the end of it. Nor are the implements of war of the medieval period. In a multi-century leap, the architect embraced the soldier of World War I to find the imagery of strength. At least two armories built in the 1920-1930 period draw on the doughboy for their inspiration. One armory is at 5200 South Cottage Grove Ave., the other is the Illinois National Guard armory at North Avenue and Kedzie. (See chapter on Statuary Alcoves for another example.)

ffice Bldg.
07 N. Broadway

1

2

3

4

5

6

7

1,2,3,4,5,6. Conrad Hilton Hotel,
720 S. Michigan Ave.
7,8,9. 233 N. DeWitt Ct.

8

9

10

11

12

14

13

15

16

10,11,15. 233 N. DeWitt Ct.

12. Powhatan Apartments,
1648 E. 50th St.

13. 4707 N. Broadway St.

14. Century Bldg.,
202 S. State St.

16. Armory, 5200 Cottage Grove Blvd.

17. 454 Winnetka Ave.,
Winnetka

18,19. Conrad Hilton Hotel,
720 S. Michigan Ave.

18   19

17

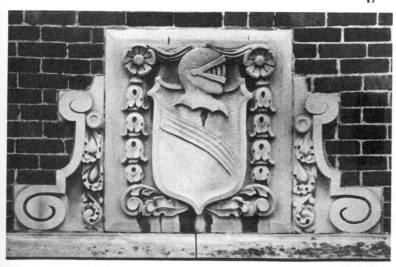

20

21

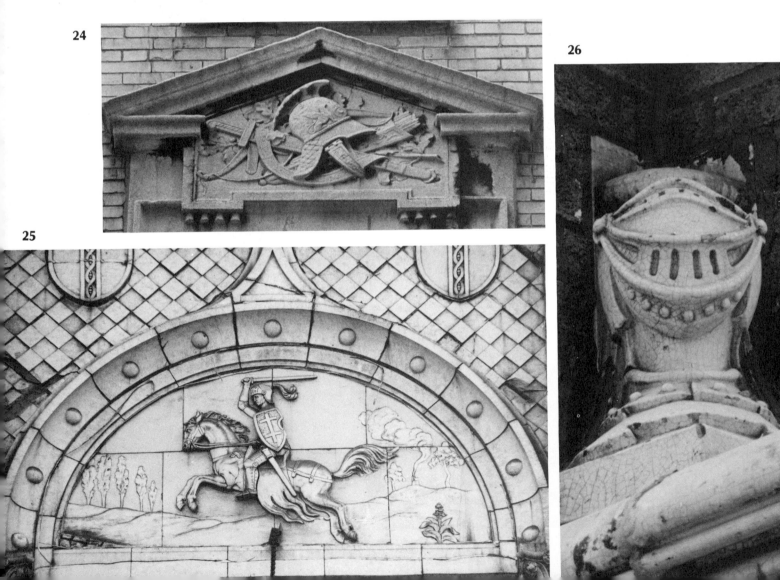

24

25

26

22 **23**

28

29

30

29,30,31,32. Illinois National Guard Armory, Kedzie and North Ave.
33. Dearborn Plaza Hotel, 1030 N. Dearborn St.
34,35. Armory, 5200 S. Cottage Grove Blvd.
36. Richmont Hotel, 162 E. Ontario St.
37. Insurance Center Bldg., 330 S. Wells St.

31

32

34

33

35

36   37

The Eagle

It is fair to say that if the bald eagle had not been adopted as the central element of our national seal in 1783, we would see less of it as a decorative ornament in our architecture. Of course its major use is on buildings of government, but don't expect it to perch there to the exclusion of all other structures. Our national symbol may be seen on banks, office buildings, schools and even garages. Designers must have thought the eagle gave the buildings it guards an aura of strength, sternness of purpose, and of being in the public interest. At the same time, it represents loyalty, patriotism and honor. In most, but certainly not all, cases, the eagle is the central focus of a building's ornament. Seldom is it an obscure design element.

Mies Van der Rohe enunciated the architectural truth, "Less is more." To some lesser mortals, "More is better" appears to be a more congenial concept, at least where the eagle is concerned. On the two-story storefront building at 703 East Sheridan, the eagle design is repeated more than 20 times along the facade and around the Halsted Street entrance. Multiple uses of a handsome eagle motif are employed on a building at 5200 West Chicago Ave.

The eagle as a symbol dates to 3000 B.C. Chaldeans envisioned the eagle as the "servant of the sun" and a symbol of immortality. The bald eagle seal designed by William Barton of Philadelphia under the direction of Charles Thomson, Secretary of the Congress, became our nation's symbol when the official seal was approved in 1783.

In Chicago architectural ornament, the eagle's styling ranges from majestic to ugly. As with all symbols — human and animal — the imperfect skills of the artist/designer often resulted in a bird that is out of proportion, distorted in position or given impossible anatomical capabilities. Notwithstanding, the eagle presents us with one of the more attractive elements of architectural ornament.

Armory, Seneca and Chicago Ave.

1

1. 5254 N. Clark St.
2. Hahn Bldg.,
   1609 Orrington Ave., Evanston
3. 141 W. Jackson St.
4. Illinois National Guard Armory,
   Kedzie and North Ave.
5. 1 N. LaSalle St.
6. Eagle Bldg.,
   1554 Howard St.
7. Continental Bank Bldg.,
   231 S. LaSalle St.

2

3

4

5

6

7

8

9   **10**

11

12

13

15

19

16

18

17

20

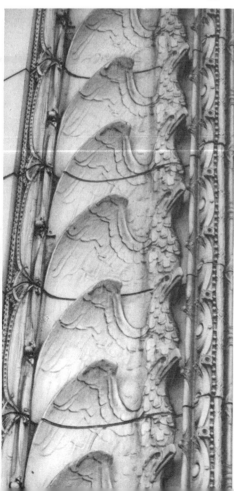

21

22

23

24

25

26

27

24,28. 150 Wilmette Ave, Wilmette

25. Cosmopolitan Bank, 801 N. Clark St.
(Now located at parking lot entrance)

26. 123 W. Madison St.

27. U.S. Post Office,
Lake Forest

29. Chicago Club,
81 E. Van Buren St. (Michigan Ave. side)

30. 4400 S. Archer Ave.

29

28

30

Barnyard and Ranch

It follows that as "hog butcher to the world" Chicago would have its share of domestic animals among its collection of architectural ornament. Such gems of ornament include "Sherman," the 1899 prizewinning steer whose sculptured head adorns the old entrance to the Chicago Stock Yards, now standing as a landmark representing those days of Chicago's greatness. Other steer heads decorate the former Portland Cement Associaton building at 515 N. Dearborn. And, on an obscure two-story building at 913 Chicago Ave., in Evanston, in red terra cotta, is the most splendid steer head of all.

The decline of Chicago as a meat packing capital has also seen the demolition of many elements of barnyard ornament. Still, those pieces that remain tell something about Chicago's history in a way that cannot be found in textbooks.

The barnyard doesn't escape the architect's symbology. The buchranium, the skull of an ox over whose horns is draped an ornamental rope, is an occasional element of ornament. It is drawn from Greek and Roman architecture. Variations of this bit of symbology may be found on the facade of the Art Institute, the Women's Athletic Club at 626 N. Michigan Ave., 3080 North Lincoln Ave, and elsewhere.

In the case of the barnyard and ranch, symbolism is drawn less from ancient sources than from the contemporary, where the symbol is used to portray what business is transacted under that particular roof. Domestic barnyard and ranch scenes are represented on the old Mercantile Exchange Building at 300 W. Washington (now Material Service Corporation headquarters) and the old Stockyards Inn (demolished, but the splendid terra cotta entrance has been moved a short distance south to 4200 S. Halsted). In the case of the latter, the vaquero and stockman graced the entrance, and they are represented here on these pages.

Blackstone Hotel
636 S. Michigan Ave.

43

1

2

3

1. Casa Bonita Apartments,
   7348 N. Ridge Rd.
2. Old Daily News Bldg.,
   2 N. Riverside Plaza
3. 3080 N. Lincoln Ave.
4. 4707 N. Broadway St.
5. Materials Service Corp. Bldg.,
   (old Mercantile Exchange), 300 W. Washington St.
6. Old Stockyards Inn entrance,
   now at 4200 S. Halsted St.
7,9. Womens Athletic Club,
   626 N. Michigan Ave.
8. Art Institute,
   S. Michigan Ave. and E. Adams St.

4

5

6

7

8

9

11

10,11,12. Materials Service Corp. Bldg.,
(old Mercantile Exchange),
300 W. Washington St.

13. Manufacturers Bank,
1200 N. Ashland Ave.

14. Former Portland Cement Bldg.,
515 N. Dearborn St.

15. Civic Tower Bldg.,
32 W. Randolph St.

16. 913 Chicago Ave., Evanston

17. Wabash Ave. and Superior St.

13

14

15

16

17

18

19

20

21

18,19,25,26. Old Stockyards Inn entrance, (now at 4200 S. Halsted St.)

20,21. 520 N. Michigan Ave.

22. Armory, 5200 S. Cottage Grove Blvd.

23. "General Sherman," On Old Stockyards Gate, 4100 s. Halsted St.

24. Board of Trade Bldg., 141 W. Jackson St.

22

23

24

25

26

Contemporary Ornament

Everyone, consciously or unconsciously, appreciates good design. No matter how untrained the eye, the human spirit is able to distinguish good design from bad, appreciate the good and be warmed by it. There is an important corollary to this truth. It is that every architect is an artist. No matter how mundane or pedestrian the structure to which the architect puts his hand, he instinctively, even almost by compulsion, gives it some artistic expression. This extends beyond the artistic satisfaction he derives from the arrangements of geometric patterns he works out with glass, steel and concrete.

The artistic expression referred to most surely does not include such corporate bows to the arts as are represented in the Picasso sculpture in the Daley Plaza, the Calder stabile at the Federal Center Plaza or the Chagall at the First National Plaza. Rather, in this chapter are shown examples of the architect/designer's own expressions, which lift his glass—steel—concrete patterns out of the cold and boring and give them a sense of humanity, reality and a human-oriented scale. The architect breathes life into his structure by locating a piece of sculpture within clear view of the building's visitors or passersby.

Chicago abounds in this architectural artistic expression. It is a part of the architectural style that has evolved since the end of World War II. Shown in this chapter are just four examples of this phenomenon. Dozens more are located throughout the city.

1. Jewish Federation Bldg.,
   1 S. Franklin St.
2. Parking Garage,
   11 W. Wacker Dr.
3. Dickens Bldg.,
   13 W. Grand Ave.

American Dental Association Bldg.,
11 E. Chicago Ave.

1

2

3

Grotesquery

The grotesque in architectural ornamentation is thought to have its origins in paganism where designs combining the worst of man, animal, fish, bird and demon were conceived as talismen capable of warding off evil spirits. The cathedrals of Europe abound with grotesques. It is plausible that the Christian authorities allowed the artisans to include grotesque figures in their ornament lest they lose these artisans — only just converted from paganism — for other essential construction. The same may be said of the misericords that adorned the pews of chapels and cathedrals of early Christian Europe. The gargoyle on many a religious structure served a utilitarian purpose. Extending out beyond the body of the building, the gargoyle's mouth carried rainwater out from the building's wall.

Lest you expect the grotesque to be limited to Gothic houses of worship, stop. Architects and designers halt at no resource in their search for ornament with which to decorate their buildings. Thus the grotesque, in all of its manifestations, may be found on every kind of structure — office building, printing plant or garage. Curiously, the ugliness of the ornament, carried to the point that it is visually rejected by the viewer, does not seem to have inhibited the architect. Rather, in some cases, such as the Daily News Building courtyard (Randolph Street and the river), the 203 N. Wabash Building and the Womens Athletic Club (626 N. Michigan), the designer seems to believe that uglier is better.

Although north European paganism first comes to mind when considering sculpture of the grotesque, Egyptian and Greek mythology contribute their share. The latter includes the chimera, a fire-eating monster with the head of a lion, the body of a goat and the tail of a serpent. The winged, four-legged predator seems to provide the architect artist with the most satisfyingly frightening subject for ornament.

1145 W. Lunt Ave.

1

2

4

3

5

1,5. 4750 N. Sheridan Rd.
2. 5709 N. Clark St.
3. 451 W. Wrightwood Ave.
4. 443 W. Wrightwood Ave.
6. 812 N. Orleans

6

7

8

11

9

12

10

13

14

15

16

17

18

19

20

21

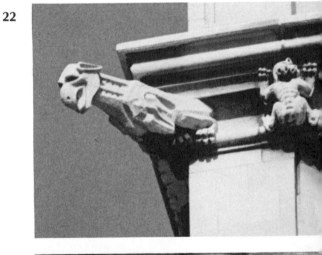

22

23

18,19,20. Manhattan Bldg.,
431 S. Dearborn St.

21,27. 203 N. Wabash Ave.

22. University Club,
76 E. Monroe St.

23. Stone Container Bldg.,
360 N. Michigan Ave.

24. 1118 N. State St.

25. Fisher Bldg.,
343 S. Dearborn St.

26. 746 W. Fullerton Ave.

28. Richmont Hotel,
162 E. Ontario St.

29. 664 N. Michigan Ave.

24

25

26

27

28

29

30

31

32

33

34

35

36

37

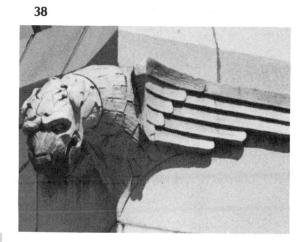

38

39

40

41

The Human Form

Architectural ornament seems to want to be explained, defined or identified by tracing the form back to its origin. The human form in ornament seems most easily explained. Parallels are found in classical Egyptian, Greek and Roman construction. The thought that the ancient pagan Celt lopped off the head of his enemy, stuck it on a pike and used it to adorn the front of his hut is too horrible to contemplate as a point of origin. And yet? The classic form gives the structure status and dignity, almost ascribing "clout" to the occupants or the contents.

The human form is most often used to decorate buildings that are somewhat public in purpose — bank, opera house, museum, stock mart, library, etc. Often the human form adorns buildings that are not such institutions, but which aspire to be thought of in that way.

Michelangelo, in his mischief, included his own portrait as well as those of Dante and Biagio de Casena when he did "The Last Judgement" in the Sistine Chapel. The practice of hiding a face in architectural ornament continues in contemporary construction. The face or figure (University Club, Tree Studios) may or may not be that of an identifiable person.

In some instances, a head is grafted onto a stock body. What is hard to understand about such sculpture is that what is done is so transparent. Upon completion of the project, it must have been obvious to the sculptor, architect and building owner that the art was unsatisfactory, and yet there it stands for all to see.

Equally embarrassing are those cases where the artist was given a space to fill. His solution was to elongate or compress the human form to fill the space. The result is a distortion that, to paraphrase Frank Lloyd Wright, even vines won't cover.

4660 N. Sheridan

61

1

2

3

4

5

8

6   7

9

10

11

12

9. Commonwealth Edison substation, 125 N. Dearborn St.
10. 4852 N. Sheridan Rd.
11. Continental Hotel, 505 N. Michigan Ave. (old Medinah Club)
12. Reebie Storage Bldg., 2325 N. Clark St.
13. Lawson YMCA, 30 W. Chicago Ave.
14. 10 W. Elm St.
15. Lakeview Branch, Chicago Public Library, 640 W. Belmont St.
16. Chicago Board of Trade Bldg., 141 W. Jackson St.
17. 6740 N. Sheridan Rd.

3

14

15

16

17

18

19

23

18. Woods Theater Bldg.,
54 W. Randolph St. (Dearborn side)
19,20,21,22. LaSalle Hotel,
LaSalle and Madison St. (demolished)
23,24. Conrad Hilton Hotel,
720 S. Michigan Ave.
25. La Salle St. Station,
143 W. Van Buren St (demolished)

20

21

22

25

24

26

29

27

28

26,27,28. Aragon Ballroom,
      Lawrence and Broadway St.
29,30,31,32,33 University Club,
      76 E. Monroe St.

30

31

32

33

34

35

36

37

38

40

41

39

42

43

44

45

45

4

43,44,45. 203 N. Wabash Ave.
46. 65 E. South Water St.
47,48. Hoover Estate,
1801 Green Bay Rd., Highland Park
49. 123 W. Madison St.
50. Dearborn Plaza Hotel,
1020 N. Dearborn St.
51. 147 W. Burton Pl.

47

48

 49

 50

51

52

53

54

55

56

62

61

61. Lewis Tower,
    820 N. Michigan Ave.
62,63. Kemper Insurance Bldg.,
    20 N. Wacker Dr.
64,65,66. Stone Container Bldg.,
    360 N. Michigan Ave.
67. 64 E. Lake St.
68. 4729 N. Broadway St.
69. Powhatan Apartments,
    1648 E. 50th St.

64

65

63

69

67

68

66

57

58

59

52,55,56. Willoughby Tower,
8 S. Michigan Ave.
53,54. Tree Studios
9 E. Ontario St.
57,58. Tree Studios,
4 E. Ohio St.
59. 190 N. State St.
60. 520 W. Armitage St.

60

Sculpture in Series

There is an ornamental phenomenon in which sculpture is arranged in a series to tell a story. In at least two cases—333 N. Michigan and 1 N. LaSalle—the piers (walls between windows) are used to carry a sequence of sculpture that relate to one another in narrative form. In the case of the 333 Building, the approximate site of Fort Dearborn, the sculpture appears to portray the evacuation of the fort. On the Michigan Avenue facade, all figures are facing south in the direction of the evacuation of the fort's residents as they headed for Fort Detroit via the southern end of Lake Michigan. They were massacred at what is approximately 22nd Street, the general area of McCormick Place.

In the case of the One N. LaSalle Building, the sculpture portrays the French explorers at the time of LaSalle. Legend—most surely manufactured by some canny real estate developer—has it that LaSalle camped near the site of this building.

A notable example of sculpture in series is the four panels above the entrance to the Marquette Building, 140 S. Dearborn. These bronze panels in high relief were designed by Hermon A. MacNeil. Quotes from Marquette's journal appear below three of the panels. The fourth quote, under the panel portraying Marquette's reinterment, is from the narrative of Father Claudius Dablon.

Equally interesting are a series of seven illustrations along the facade of the Franklin Building at 720 S. Dearborn. The illustrations, on a building on Chicago's old Printing House Row, appropriately tell the story of the process of printing, and are almost in the genre of old Saturday Evening Post covers.

These illustrations are not sculptures but mosaics of interestingly-laid, colored terra cotta tile. An eighth and much larger mosaic appears over the former main entrance to the building. With a sense of humor that is a delight, the complete printing process is shown is one illustration entitled, "The First Impression." Look for the printing pressman in the background. He may be seen, with arm draped over the press, in full yawn.

Sculpture in a series is most frequently to be found in incised or intaglio form on building facades of concrete. Banks are likely candidates for series sculptures.

The essence of restrained fine design is expressed in two pieces of sculpture on either side of the entrance to the Anti-Cruelty Society Building at 157 W. Grand. A male figure on the left, facing the entrance, is watering a horse. A female figure on the right succors a cat and dog.

Architectural ornament is not without its tragedies. A series of three free-standing bronze statues by Milton Horn once ornamented the National Association of Parents and Teachers Building at 700 Rush St. The statues are entitled "The Teacher," "The Mother" and "The Father." One of them was stolen in 1981. By great good fortune, Horn had the original molds and the statue was cast again. The three statues are now no longer on the outside of the building but have been relocated inside the Association's offices. They are pictured in this chapter as they originally appeared.

Marquette Bldg.
140 S. Dearborn St.

1

2

3

1,2,3,4,5,6,7,8. Franklin Bldg.,
720 S. Dearborn St.
9,10. 215 E. Chestnut St.

4

8

9

10

11

12

13

14

15

1

17

18

11,12,13,14,15,16. Dr. John B. Murphy Memorial,
50 E. Erie St.
17,18,19,20 Marquette Bldg ,
140 S. Dearborn St.

"TO FOLLOW THOSE WATERS * * * WHICH WILL
HENCEFORTH LEAD VS INTO STRANGE LANDS"

"IN VAIN I SHOWED THE CALVMET * * * TO EXPLAIN
THAT WE HAD NOT COME AS ENEMIES"

19

20

"PASSING TWO LEAGVES VP THE RIVER WE RESOLVED
TO WINTER THERE * * BEING DETAINED BY MY ILLNESS"

"THE DE PROFVNDIS WAS INTONED * * * THE BODY
WAS THEN CARRIED TO THE CHVRCH"

21

22

23

2

24

28

29

27

21,22,23. Bismark Hotel,
111 W. Randolph St.

24,25. Union Hall,
4217 S. Halsted St.

26,27,28,29. 201 Tower Bldg.,
201 N. Wells St.

30

34

31

32

35   36   37   38

30,31,32,33 Pioneer Bank,
    4000 W. North Ave.
34,35,36,37,38. Three Arts Club,
    1300 N. Dearborn St.

33

39

40

41

ART IS
TE IMIA
TION
OF
NA
TURE IN
HER

MANNER
OF
OPERA
TION

42

39,40 U.S. Post Office,
1101 Davis St., Evanston

41,42,43,44,45,46,47 Former Continental Can
R&D Bldgs, 1350 W. 76th St.

44

43

46

45

47

49

48

51

50

48,49,50,51. 1300 E. Hyde Park Ave.

52,53,54. Tree Studios,
3 E. Ontario St.

55,56,57. National Congress of Parents
and Teachers Bldg., 700 N. Rush St.

52

57

55

56

53

54

58

59

60   **61**   **62**   **63**

67

66

65

58,59,60,61,62,63,64. 333 N. Michigan Ave.
65,66,67. 520 N. Michigan Ave.

64

68

69

72

70   71

73

74

75

76

77

68,69 Anti-Cruelty Society Bldg.,
157 W. Grand Ave.
70,71,72,73,74,75,76,77. 1 N. LaSalle St.

Statuary Alcoves

The statuary alcove is an element of architectural ornament but it is sometimes something else: an amusement. Too often it represents space reserved for a statue that isn't there—sort of like an empty chair at a dinner party.

In two instances the alcove amused because it contains a surprising piece of statuary. In one alcove of the splendidly designed Gothic St. Luke's Episcopal Church in Evanston, there is the figure of a World War I doughboy. The covered walkway between manse and church is dedicated to members of the congregation who died in World War I, which explains the figure. In the other, in an alcove in Market Square in Lake Forest, is a statue completely out of place with the period of the structure—contemporary sculpture is on a building of the Tudor period.

For the most part, in American design the statuary alcove seems to have been intended for a piece of statuary that never made its way to the alcove. The empty alcove causes speculation that the building's original design called for the sculpture, but when the building was finished there was no money left for the statuary. There can be no doubt that buildings such as the Lincoln Tower at 75 E. Wacker, with its row of four empty statuary alcoves across the front, looks jealously upon such structures as the Rockefeller Chapel at the University of Chicago which carries eleven lifesize religious figures in alcoves above its entrance. All statuary-starved buildings must envy the Hotel de Ville in Brussels, which has over 400 figures in alcoves going up the four stories of its facade.

St. Luke's Church
Lee and Hinman Aves., Evanston.

1

3

4

2

5

1. National Guard Armory,
   Broadway and Rosedale St.
2. R.R. Donnelley plant,
   2223 S. King Dr.
3. 19 E. Delaware St.
4. Sheridan Plaza Hotel,
   Sheridan and Wilson St.
5. Bankers Bldg.,
   105 W. Adams St. (Clark side)

6

7

8

6. Lewis Tower,
   820 N. Michigan Ave.
7. Wrigley Bldg.,
   400 N. Michigan Ave.
8. 3021 N. Lincoln Ave.
9. Market Square, Lake Forest
10. Birren & Son Mortuary,
    1356 W. Wellington St.
11. Racquet Club,
    1365 N. Dearborn St.
12. Lincoln Tower,
    75 E. Wacker Dr.

10

9

11

12

Vasery

Probably no element of achitectural ornament is more incongruous than the Grecian urn or vase. Although in truth it has no allegorical significance, no doubt the first image the vase calls to mind is funereal, for certainly the urn is very much an element of the cemetery monument. In most but not all instances, the vase is found along the roofline—a sitting duck for a boy with a snowball or slingshot, if he can reach that elevation. Weather, too, is the enemy of this urn or vase. Over the years, the cement or seals that have held the ornaments in place will give away, and one by one the carefully spaced vases are lost, until the roofline looks something like a child's smile that has been generously financed by the tooth fairy.

Vases or urns as they stand at the roofline are never actually vases. Even the most unaware architect or designer would not use a design that allowed the ornament to fill with water, ice or snow. The vase design has been corrupted until it has become a mere vestigial knob or decorative button. Examples of these are found in abundance. In other cases, the roofline ornament is not a vase, but a vessel holding a flame or other ornament. In a very few cases, the vase is truly that, holding an arrangement of fruits or flowers. Some of these on buildings of little consequence are magnificently done.

Most ornamental vasery is to be found on the roofline, to be sure, but there are examples throughout the city of vase designs placed elsewhere on a building's facade. In such cases, they are often much larger and more elaborate that the typical roofline ornament.

Palmer House
19 E. Monroe St.

1. 1155 E. Lunt St.
2. 3510 N. Sheridan Rd.
3. 7334 N. Clark St.
4. Wrigley Bldg.,
    400 N. Michigan Ave.
5. 4710 N. Lincoln Ave.

6

6. 3054 N. Lincoln Ave.
7,13. 4707 N. Broadway St.
8. 1164 N. Dearborn St.
9. 1607 W. Howard St.
10. 51st and Halsted St.
11. 6460 N. Sheridan Rd.
12. Dr. John B. Murphy Memorial,
    50 E. Erie St.
14,15. Hoover Estate,
    1801 Green Bay Rd., Highland Park

7

10

8

9

11

12

15

13

14

16

16. Marshall Field's,
    Market Square, Lake Forest
17. 6236 N. Broadway St.
18. 7615 N. Paulina St.
19. 742 W. Fullerton Ave.
20. Sheridan Plaza Hotel,
    Sheridan and Wilson St.
21. 1033 Davis St., Evanston
22. Dr. John B. Murphy Memorial,
    50 E. Erie St.
23. 180 N. Washington St.
24. Black Hawk Restaurant,
    139 N. Wabash Ave.
25. 5707 N. Clark St.

17

18

19

20

21

22

23

25

24

The Ubiquitous Brick

Seldom in construction do artist and artisan go one on one with each other; the case of the architect or designer and the bricklayer is an exception. Here there is no industrial arts middleman who makes a mold, does a casting or, in other ways, serves as the intermediary between artist and finished product. When the architect or designer designs ornament in brick, the bricklayer translates it exactly into what appears on the building. Here, if ever, the artisan's skills are fully on display. And here, as ever, the pedestrian walks by the finished work with little regard for the skills that went into its making.

Perhaps even some knowledgeable architectural types do not appreciate the very special skill required to lay bricks in a circle. Accordingly, few appreciate the skill it took for bricklayers to spell out the word "Police" in brick on the front of the station at 6400 N. Clark. Even greater skill was needed to recreate in brick the circular logo of the Continental Bank on the wall at Clark and Elm (now covered over).

A great many multi-story buildings have their windowless solid brick side walls broken up with patterns of brick in different colors. Few can imagine the tedium endured by the bricklayer, who lays brick after brick up this facade, all the while remembering that bricks of the second color must be precisely placed lest there be a mistake in the pattern.

The monotony of a solid brick wall broken by the pattern of different colored brick laid in a design is most certainly a fulfillment of one of the three purposes of architectural ornament—to relieve the otherwise tiresome horizontal and vertical lines of the structure.

.K. Culver Offices
26 N. Clark St.

1. 4515 N. Lincoln Ave.
2. 2772 N. Lincoln Ave.
3. 1300 E. Hyde Park Ave.
4. Bloom Township High School,
   10th and Chicago Ave., Chicago Heights
5. 5208 N. Clark St.
6. Devon Theater,
   Devon and Broadway St.
7. National Guard Armory,
   Broadway and Rosedale St.
8. 620 N. Clark St.

5

6

7

8

9

10

9. 1035 N. Clark St.
10. Police Station,
    6400 N. Clark St.
11. Continental Bank Office,
    Clark and Elm St. (now covered)
12. Washington Bldg. (old Krause Laundry),
    1215 Washington St., Wilmette
13. 913 Chicago Ave., Evanson
14. St. Andrews School,
    1710 W. Addison St.
15. Aragon Ballroom,
    Lawrence and Broadway st.
16. 1518 W. Hollywood Ave.

12

11

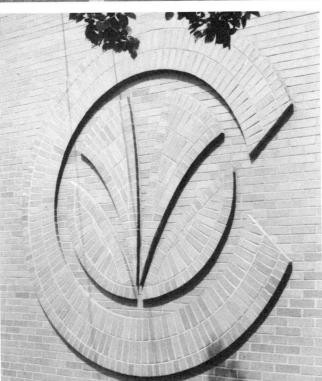

13

14

15

16

And Then There Was Sullivan

In the world of architectural ornament, Louis Sullivan (1856—1924) is unique. Whereas other architects drew on earlier art forms for their inspiration and incorporated allegorical figures and designs into their architecture, Louis Sullivan evolved a style entirely out of his own head. The combination of geometric and floral forms which were Sullivan's style are truly things of beauty. Typically, in desperate efforts to describe the Sullivan style, words such as "poetic" and "lyrical" are employed, all to no end because words are quite inadequate to provide a translation of Sullivan's designs from pictures into words.

The largest collection of Sullivan's drawings are in the Avery Library at Columbia University, given to that institution by Frank Lloyd Wright, who received them three days before Sullivan's death. No collection of drawings can match the soaring beauty of the facade of the Carson Pirie Scott & Co. Building at One S. State St. (originally the Schlesinger & Mayer Building). The last major commercial building designed by Sullivan was built in 1899. While crediting Sullivan fully for the beautiful ornament on the Carson Building, it should be noted that a Sullivan associate, George C. Elmslie, had much to do with the design of this ornament. Sullivan ornament on other Chicago Buildings has suffered. The Troescher Building on S. Wacker Drive has been torn down. Some of his ornament on the Gage Building at 18 S. Michigan Ave. has been covered over or partially obscured. His Krause Music Store on N. Lincoln Ave. remains.

Ornament of all kinds was manufactured in volume during the last half of the 19th Century and sold from catalogs. At least two such firms flourished in Chicago during that period, providing mass-produced ornament in a variety of materials, especially terra cotta. Sullivanesque designs imitating the master were incorporated into the facades of even the meanest buildings. This type of ornament abounds in Chicago. There are two ways of looking at this imitation of Sullivan. One is to view it as, perhaps, analogous to the needle trades wherein an original design is copied (read stolen) and overnight offered en masse at bargain basement prices. Conversely, one might look upon such copying of Sullivan as an act of homage paid to one of the very few—maybe even the only—original mind which applied itself to the business of architectural ornament.

One must look beyond Sullivan's writings for an explanation of the concept of his design style. His short volume, *A System of Architectural Ornament*, by its title gives rise to the thought that this, indeed, will provide insights. Not so. It is in fact a series of tortured paragraphs that give little or no help.

In every case in which Sullivan had a hand in the design of a structure, his ornament was conceived at the time the design of the building was begun. In this way, he showed that the ornament was an integral part of the building's design, not something that could be pasted on after construction or peeled off at a later date. Sullivan genuinely thought that ornament gave character to the structure on which it appeared. Curiously, while Sullivan was in the forefront of the Prairie School of Architecture, and no end of his buildings including the Wainwright Building in St. Louis, are landmarks, he is remembered as much, if not more, for his ornamental design than for his architecture. In the current Encyclopaedia Britannica, more attention is given to his ornament than to his architectural skills.

Carson, Pirie, Scott & Co.
2 S. State.

1

2

3

4

6

7

8

1. 14 W. Washington St.
2. Moody Church,
   1630 N. Clark St.
3,4,5. Troescher Bldg.,
   15 S. Wacker Dr. (demolished)
6,7,8. Getty Tomb, Graceland Cemetery,
   4001 N. Clark St.

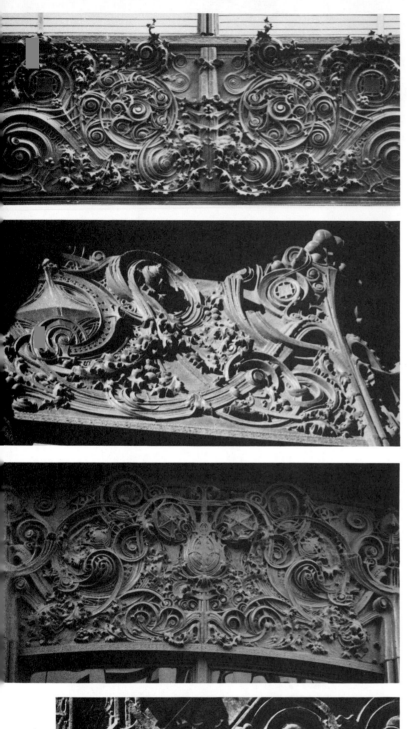

9

10

11

13

1

12

5

17

16

10

19,20,21,22,23,24,25,26. Carson, Pirie, Scott & Co.
1 S. State St.

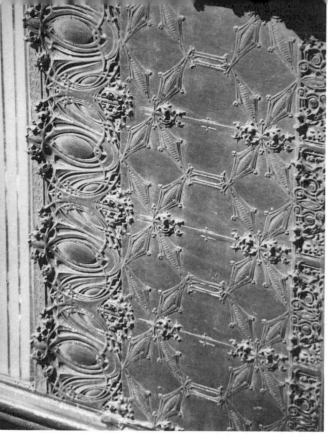

23

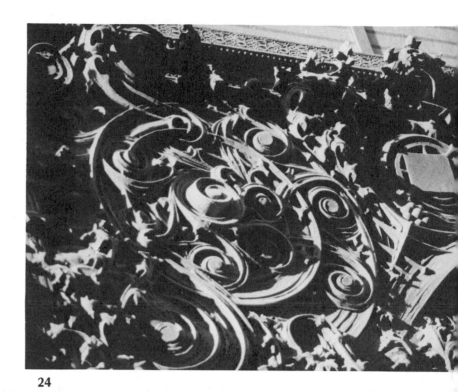

24

25

26

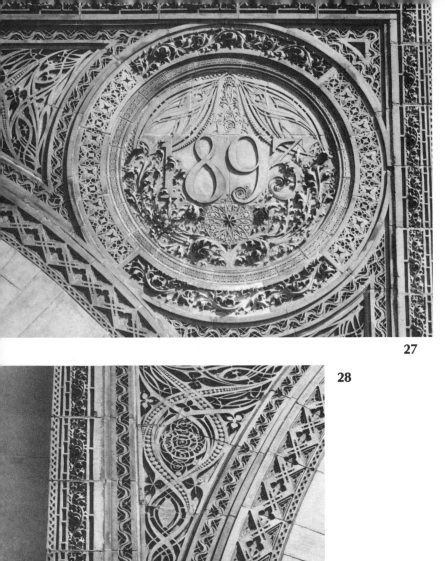

27

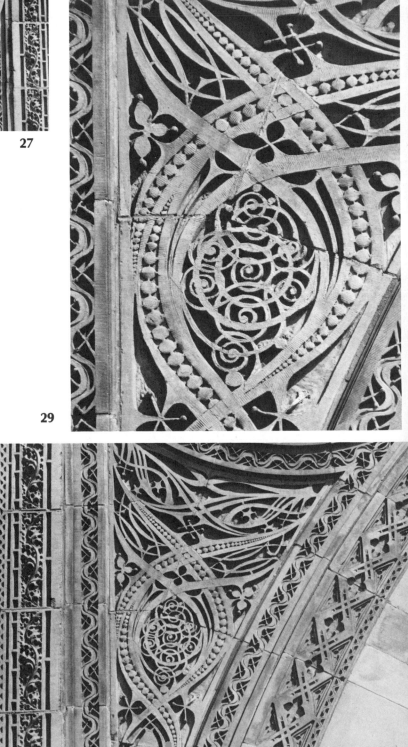

28

29

30

31

32

34

33

35

Cartouche, Oval and Circle

The cartouche, the circle and the oval are examples of the historical distances to which architects will travel in their search for symbols with which to ornament their work. The cartouche is the means the ancient Egyptian kings used for signing their names—a series of symbols enclosed within an oval. The Chinese did the same thing, but their insignia is called a "chop." The circle, a line without end, is said to represent eternity. The oval has a host of symbolic meanings.

Having embraced these forms, the architect thereupon set about embellishing them. The oval, circle or cartouche is most frequently enlarged upon on its exterior while the symbology—the more cryptic the better, it seems—is employed within the frame.

The cartouche, through the passage of time and frequent use, seems to have become the most susceptible of embellishment. It is often the central design over the entrance to a building. As with its sisters, the circle and the oval, it is often repeated again and again in the decorative elements of the building. Floral designs probably are the most frequently used, but many architects have been carried away to the extent that they have used generously endowed females or cupids or angels to provide figurative support for the cartouche. However, on occasion, the architect has also used the design in its most unadorned form. An example of this is to be found on the Knight Building, at 549 W. Randolph St.

The circle, because it lends itself so easily to repetition, often is employed with a changing inner design that runs in series. In such cases, there is an overlap between its appearance in this chapter and in the chapter, **Sculpture in Series**.

Richmont Hotel
162 E. Ontario.

1

1. Manufacturers Bank,
   1200 N. Ashland Ave.

2. Dewes House,
   503 W. Wrightwood St.

3. 1020 Davis St., Evanston

4. Fisher Bldg.,
   343 S. Dearborn St.

5. Kemper Bldg.,
   20 N. Wacker Dr. (river side)

6. 35 E. Wacker Dr.

7. 5404 N. Clark St.

8. Hahn Bldg.,
   1609 Orrington Ave., Evanston

9. Lytton Bldg.,
   14 E. Jackson St.

10. Belden Stratford Hotel,
    2300 N. Lincoln Park West

11. 222 E. Ontario St.

2

3

4

6

8

7

9

10

11

12

15

16

17

13

14

19

18

20

21

22

ANNO   DOMINI
MDCCCXCIII

23

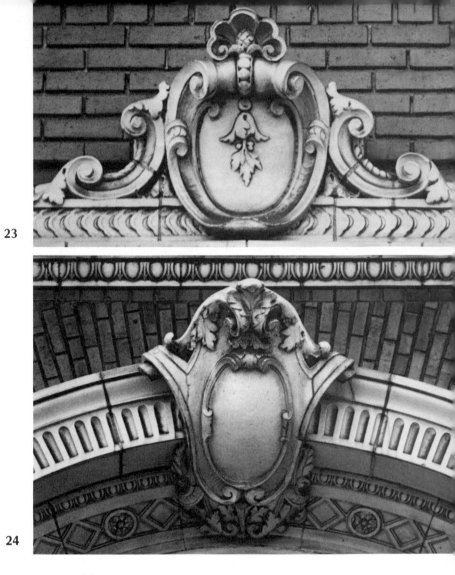

24

26

25

27

28

29

30

31

Flora, Fauna and Festoonery

Probably no elements of ornament are given over so completely to symbology as plants and animals. Almost every form of flower, leaf and stem has some cryptic meaning which the architect seems to find hilariously imaginative. Either he is sending messages to his fellow craftsmen, speaking through the symbolic code that only he and they know, or he wishes to be recognized by all who are of the "in" group. Whatever the reason, plants, animals, birds and fish, depending upon their species, have a symbolic meaning. Many of these uses of flora and fauna are so far-fetched as to be almost lost.

A search for the origins of the pelican is an example. It generally symbolizes succoring, caring, and even Christian charity. In fact, the pelican's origin as an element of symbology predates Christianity by uncounted centuries. It seems to me that often the image is employed for its intrinsic beauty, and the rationale for using it is dreamed up later, if at all. The pelican, goes the legend that accompanies the symbol, in its extremity to care for its young, fed them by stabbing its breast with its beak to feed the young with its own blood. If such is the case, perhaps Lewis Tower of the Loyola University Water Tower campus (820 N. Michigan Ave.) and the American Red Cross Building at 43 E. Ohio St. are appropriately ornamented.

To appreciate this ornament, one would unquestionably be better served by ignoring the symbology and embracing the ornament simply for its beauty of detail and its artistic quality.

The marvelously accurate reproduction, in beautiful color, of floral ornament at top and base of the pillars of the Reebie Moving & Storage Building, 233 N. Clark St., is obscured by the more spectacular Egyptian figures that stagger the eye at the building's entrance. The fresh white terra cotta vegetable ornament that surrounds the entrance of the Deming Shore Apartments at 484 W. Deming is a similar delight.

Deming Shore Apartments
484 W. Deming.

1. 199 E. Lake Shore Dr.
2. Reebie Storage Bldg.,
   2325 N. Clark St.
3. Red Cross Bldg.,
   43 E. Ohio St.
4. 1366 N. Dearborn St.

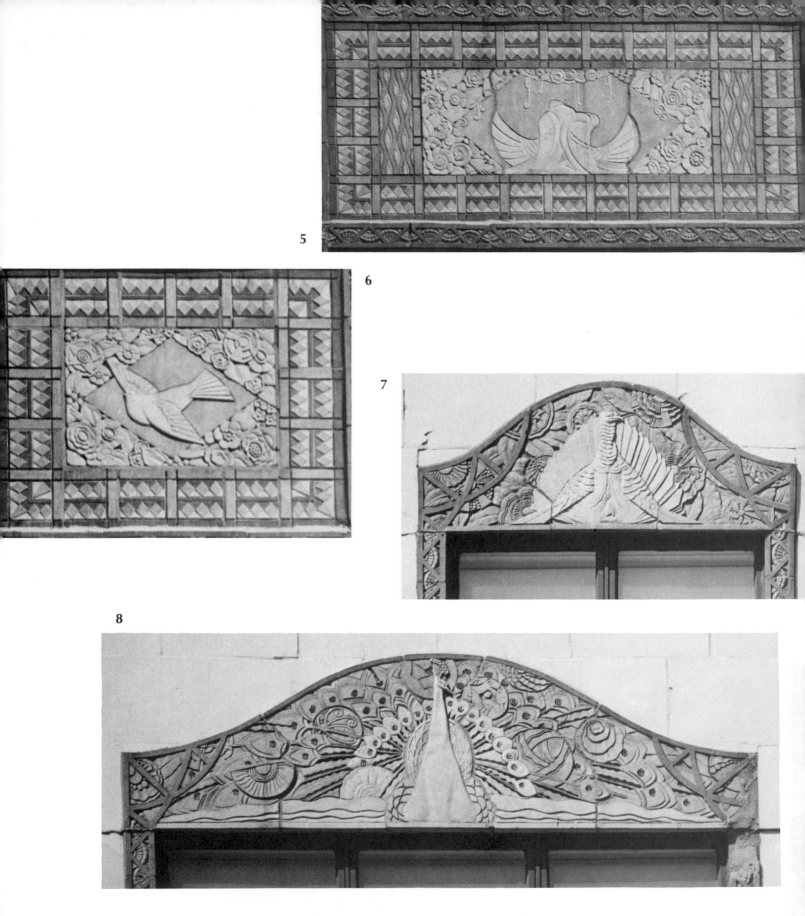

5

6

7

8

9

10

11

12

13

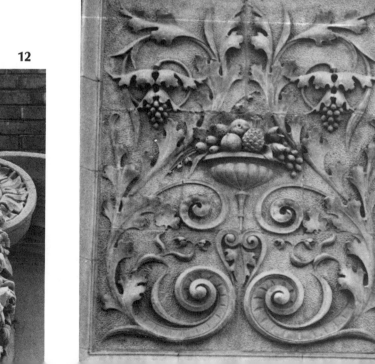

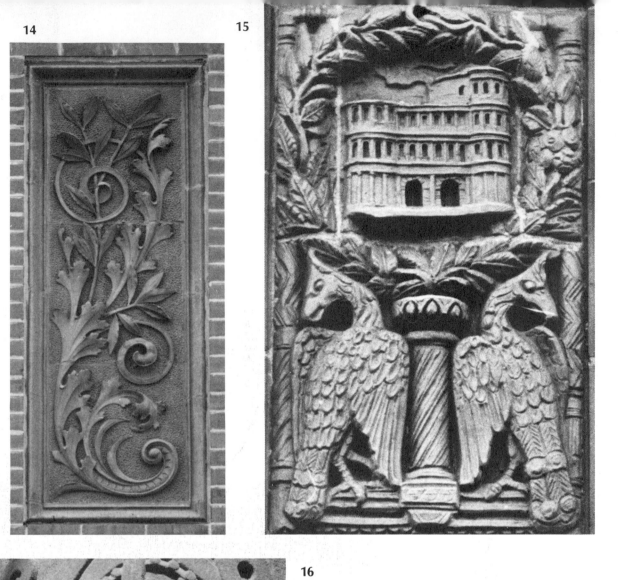

14

15

16

17

8

19

20

21

22

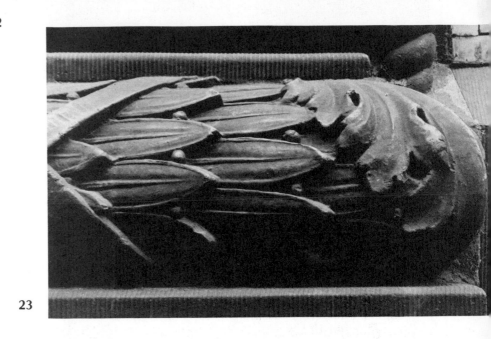

23

24

25

22. Raphael Hotel,
    201 E. Delaware Pl.
23. Marquette Bldg.,
    140 S. Dearborn St.
24. Sheridan Plaza Hotel,
    Sheridan and Wilson St.
25. Crerar Library,
    83 E. Randolph St. (demolished)
26. Unidentified
27. 209 E. Lake Shore Dr.
28. 2058 N. Cleveland Ave.
29. 180 W. Washington St.

26

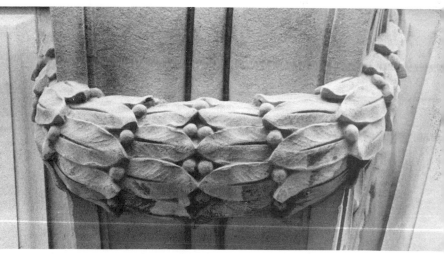

27

28

29

Pediments, Panoramas and Potpourri

Pediments and panoramas are Greek, Roman and Egyptian. The potpourri, in this chapter, is strictly the author's.

The pediment, the triangular piece over a doorway or facade in the original Greek architectural style, has gone to the rooftop with the skyscraper. It seems as though the architect thought, "Ah, here's my big chance to ornament this building in a way that will really wow them." The result is that some of the most elaborate ornament is to be found in this location, especially on buildings of classic design. Not to say that such ornament is limited to buildings in the classic mode. At once some truly splendid and some terribly trashy ornament is to be found on building pediments in Chicago. On occasion, the design may have been well intentioned but the execution went astray.

Enormous effort has gone into the sculpture of some pediments and panoramas and, being at the roofline of our skyscrapers, they are in the substratosphere where few people notice them or can see them even if the sculpture is the object of a search. An example is the sculptured frieze of the Greek olympic games at the roofline of the Illinois Athletic Club Building at 112 S. Michigan Ave. The heroic effect may be seen in full view because of the open space afforded by the park across the street. Nevertheless, it is probable that the sculpture is seldom noticed, being overshadowed by the Art Institute approximately across the way.

A panoramic gem little noticed, perhaps because like Poe's purloined letter it is in full view and close at hand, is found on a one story storefront at 6460 N. Sheridan. It is a colored terra cotta Chicago skyline as seen from the lake.

Egyptian panorama sculpture (bas relief) is mightily represented around three visible sides of the south wing of the Continental Hotel at 505 N. Michigan Ave. Originally this was the Medinah Athletic Club, which explains the Egyptian motif.

Potpourri is the grand melange of all the examples of ornament that either do not warrant classification and inclusion as separate chapters, or warrant classification but are too few in number to make that practical. The one exception is the scallop shell, of which I have included only a few examples not because there are so few available, but because there are so many. It seems almost that whenever the architect felt the need to insert some ornament in his work, he reached for his file of shell designs. The result is that this ancient symbol of birth, life, regeneration and fertility may be seen everywhere—in good design and bad, and in every medium.

But this potpourri presents just a few of the hundreds, no, thousands, of bits of Chicago architectural ornament waiting to be viewed. Chicago is perhaps the richest city in America in architectural ornament. And, as in its sister cities, this ornament is largely unappreciated. Perhaps by gathering these examples into a corner of this volume, those who read it will be stimulated to look up—to see, enjoy and appreciate the architectural ornament that has been incorporated into Chicago's buildings, at least in part, for our pleasure.

Aragon Ballroom
Lawrence and Broadway

1

1. Holy Name Cathedral Convent Bldg.,
   30 N. Superior St.
2,8. Rookery Bldg.,
   LaSalle and Adams St.
3. 2534 W. Fullerton Ave.
4. 919 W. Armitage St.
5. Van Buren Bldg.,
   210 W. Van Buren St.
6. Continental Bank,
   231 S. LaSalle St.
7. Marshall Field's,
   Randolph and State St.
9. 1033 N. Clark St.

2

4

3

6

7

8

9

10

11

13

12

15

14

16

17

18

19

18,24. Continental Hotel,
505 N. Michigan Ave. (old Medinah Club)
19. 4040 N. Sheridan Rd.
20. 748 W. Fullerton Ave.
21. Narragansett Apartments,
1640 E. 50th St.
22. Illinois Athletic Club,
112 S. Michigan Ave.
23. St. Joseph Hospital,
2900 N. Lake Shore Dr.
25. 3640 N. Halsted St.

20

21

22

23

24

25

26.

26. Aragon Ballroom,
Lawrence and Touhy St.
27. Germania Club,
1536 N. Clark St.
28. 2516 W. Fullerton Ave.
29. 718 S. Dearborn St.
30. Carbide & Carbon Bldg.,
230 N. Michigan Ave.
(South Water St. entrance)
31. Rand McNally Store.,
23 E. Madison Ave.
32. Unidentified
33. 901 Ridge Rd., Wilmette

27.

28.

29

30

31

32

33

34

35

34,35,36. 6460 N. Sheridan Rd.
37. 2324 W. Devon St.
38. 129 N. Wabash St.
39. Marquette Bldg.,
140 S. Dearborn St.
(footplate on revolving door)
40. Field Museum,
S. Lake Shore Dr. and E. Roosevelt Rd.
41. 1520 N. State St.
42. 122 S. Michigan Ave.

36

37

38

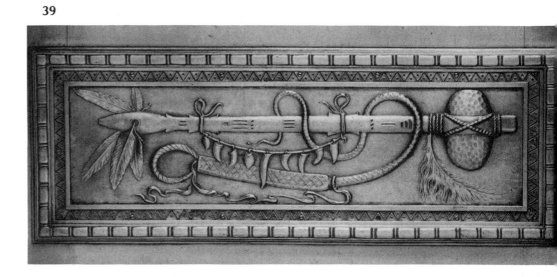

39

41

42

40